IMAGES
of Sport

CARDIFF
DEVILS

One of the most influential players in Cardiff Devils' history, Steve Moria joined the Welsh club in the summer of 1988, and was still among the side's leading scorers in the 2000/01 season. He is pictured during that latest campaign, which saw him reach his fortieth birthday and benefit from a testimonial match. He had spent three seasons away from Cardiff between 1992 and 1995 – two at Blackburn and one at Swindon.

IMAGES
of Sport

CARDIFF
DEVILS

Compiled by
Andrew Weltch

TEMPUS

First published 2001
Copyright © Andrew Weltch 2001

Tempus Publishing Limited
The Mill, Brimscombe Port,
Stroud, Gloucestershire, GL5 2QG

ISBN 0 7524 2257 X

Typesetting and origination by
Tempus Publishing Limited
Printed in Great Britain by
Midway Colour Print, Wiltshire

Contents

Acknowledgements

This book would not have been possible without the generous help of Richard Murray and Anthony Beer, who between them provided me with thousands of photographs to choose from, and much helpful advice as well. Richard was the Devils' official photographer for many years and is responsible for around half the photographs in the book. Anthony's encyclopaedic knowledge of the club's history also proved invaluable for checking elusive facts.

Others who kindly provided material for the book include: Bob Reed, Trevor Benbrook, Lynne McEwan, Rachel Waters, Whitbread Beer Co. and Western Mail and Echo.

Special thanks are due to Gren for permission to reproduce his cartoon from the *South Wales Echo*, Simon Potter, editor of *Powerplay* magazine, Terry Phillips of the *South Wales Echo*, Stewart Roberts, editor of *The Ice Hockey Annual*, Alan Edmunds, editor of *Wales on Sunday*, and Andy French of the Devils. Thanks also to Steve Lewis of the Sports Bookshop in Cardiff for suggesting the idea of an *Images of Sport* on Cardiff Devils, James Howarth of Tempus Publishing for agreeing, and project editor Kate Wiseman for making sense of it all.

Finally, thanks to my family, Ruth, Richard and Sarah, for tolerating a house full of hockey pictures for six months.

Andrew Weltch
September 2001

Introduction

Cardiff Devils played a major role in the development of British ice hockey at the end of the twentieth century. Their audacious signing of top players from more established clubs paved the way for the return of fully professional hockey in Britain, and their meteoric rise set the standards for the new clubs established in the late 1980s and 1990s.

Wales was a late developer in ice hockey terms. Although Britain had won Olympic gold as long ago as 1936, and the Oxford-Cambridge Varsity match dates back to 1885, it was 1974 before Wales had a hockey team at Deeside in North Wales, and a further twelve years before the sport reached the south.

Devils made their home debut in November 1986, when a capacity crowd of 2,500 packed the new Wales National Ice Rink to see Cardiff skate away to a 32-0 destruction of hapless Ashfield Islanders. The big win and the enthusiastic support were to set the tone for the coming seasons, as player-manager John Lawless led his team to Division One of the Heineken League by their second season and the Premier Division two years later.

That first campaign in the top flight saw success beyond anyone's expectations, as the newcomers won the league title, and then beat mighty Murrayfield Racers to win the showpiece Wembley final in a penalty shoot-out, live in front of the BBC *Grandstand* cameras. Such was the nail-biting tension of the occasion that the producers delayed their coverage of the world snooker championship to stay with the hockey until Tony Hand's miss gave Cardiff their play-off title. Further league, play-off and even European success would follow, but there was never quite a moment to match the remarkable achievements of that 1989/90 season.

The departure of Lawless for the top job at newly-formed Manchester Storm, with their arena seven times the capacity of Cardiff's, in the summer of 1995, marked the end of an era for the Welsh club; a year later the collapse of the British League, and establishment of the ambitious new Superleague, was the start of another.

The league spoke of plans for expansion and arenas of at least 5,000 capacity for all teams within a few years. Yet this, like the promise of developing young British talent, was not realised. The standard of hockey was certainly higher, but the dominance of imports increased costs, and some teams struggled to meet them. Cardiff experienced changes of ownership and threats of closure before everything finally fell apart in the summer of 2001.

Much had been made of a planned new arena in Cardiff Bay, with a capacity of 7,000. Bigger crowds, it was argued, would bring more revenue and allow the club to continue to compete at the top level; staying in the small city centre rink was creating losses of £250,000 a year. The trouble was that there were usually hundreds of spare seats in the little rink, and filling a bigger arena would be no easy task.

After a superb late season run in spring 2001, Devils claimed runners-up spot in the Superleague, but failed to progress in the play-offs. When the season ended doubts arose over the club's future. The company which owned the club went into liquidation, with players claiming they were owed thousands of pounds in unpaid wages.

As the summer wore on, the survival of Superleague hockey in Cardiff seemed less likely, and gradually almost the entire playing squad and other staff moved on. New owners entered the Devils name in the lower level British National League and put together a new team from scratch in less than two weeks.

However, many fans claimed the new owners had links with the previous company, and launched a campaign of boycott and protests to get the outstanding player debts paid. As the 2001/2 season got under way, Cardiff's ice hockey community was in the grip of a damaging split, which threatened the future of the sport in South Wales.

By bringing together more than 230 photographs, cuttings and other images, this book aims to provide an informal review of the club's first fifteen seasons. It is not intended to be a comprehensive history, but my hope is that the following pages will provide a timely reminder of many of the faces and events which shaped the Cardiff Devils story from 1986 to 2001.

Andrew Weltch
September 2001

One
Early Days
1986-87

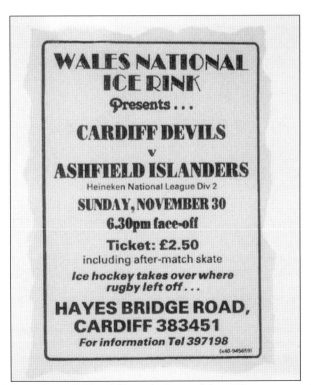

WALES NATIONAL ICE RINK

Presents . . .

CARDIFF DEVILS

v

ASHFIELD ISLANDERS

Heineken National League Div 2

SUNDAY, NOVEMBER 30

6.30pm face-off

Ticket: £2.50

including after-match skate

Ice hockey takes over where rugby left off . . .

HAYES BRIDGE ROAD, CARDIFF 383451

For information Tel 397198

(x40-9456591)

The newspaper advertisement for Cardiff Devils' home debut. The new team had already played five away games while they waited for their rink to be ready, winning four and drawing one, but even that successful record was to be eclipsed by their first game in Cardiff.

Sunday 30th November
HEINEKEN LEAGUE
DIVISION TWO

Face-off 6.30

CARDIFF

DEVILS

≡ICE HOCKEY CLUB≡
V
ASHFIELD ISLANDERS

Tonight's Match Sponsored by   SOUTH WALES WINDOWS

PROGRAMME 60p

WALES NATIONAL
ICE RINK
CARDIFF

Hayes Bridge Road,
Cardiff CF1 2GH.

The programme cover for Devils' first home match against Ashfield Islanders in the Midlands section of British League Division Two. Player-manager John Lawless later commented: 'I had thought maybe 1,000 fans would come and see us, maybe not. When we came out to a full house of 2,500, I don't think any of the players could believe it!' The crowd were not disappointed – Cardiff crushed the young amateurs 32-0.

The first season squad, from left to right, back row: Norman Jaques (equipment manager), Bill Taylor, Glen Haley, Paul Farmer, Perry Olivier, Paul Morganti. Front row: Mike Jaques, Bleddyn Davies, John Lawless, Mike Kellond, Steve Oliver, Max Thurgood.

Crunch! One of Cardiff's three permitted imports was hard-hitting Canadian defender Bill Taylor, seen here during a 14-2 win over Bristol Phantoms. A fireman and professional hunter back home, he was known to fans as 'Grizzly' and was much missed when his season was interrupted by a dislocated shoulder in a challenge match at Swindon Wildcats in February 1987.

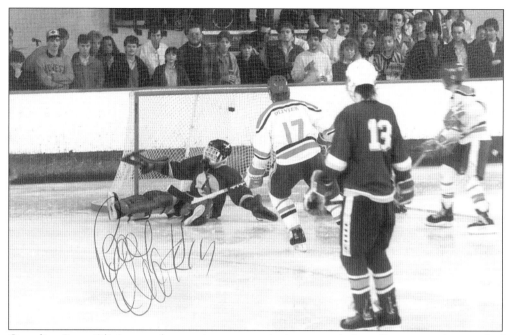

Canadian Perry Olivier was the team's top scorer in league and play-off games, with a total of 80 goals and 72 assists in 15 matches. Here he fires past the stranded Ashfield netminder during Islanders' second visit to Cardiff in April. With no home ice, Ashfield had to play all their games away. This time they lost 35-0.

Player-manager John Lawless completed the trio of imports, and was almost as prolific as Olivier. Playing one game less, he scored 78 goals and 73 assists. He is seen here performing his trademark goal celebration – 'shooting' the scoreboard with his stick as the gun.

The visit of North Wales team Deeside Dragons promised the first really competitive match of the season. Fans queued for up to two hours to book their tickets for the big game, which ended 3-3 – the only point Cardiff dropped in the league all season.

When Lawless contracted hepatitis, another Canadian, Mike Urquhart (pictured on the right alongside Paul Morganti), was recruited. On Urquhart's debut, a challenge match at Swindon, Bill Taylor dislocated his shoulder, and Urquhart saw out the season with the Welsh club.

The home game against Trafford Tigers (the B-team of Division One Trafford Metros) was a typically one-sided affair. *Above:* Glen Haley scores one of Cardiff's 28 goals – Trafford netted one in reply. *Below:* In the same match, Perry Olivier controls the puck, while Max Thurgood awaits a pass.

John Lawless refused to let a bout of hepatitis keep him out of action for long. He is pictured (left) with his end-of-season 'play-off beard'. The side's only Welshman in their first season was teenager Bleddyn Davies (right), who scored 6 goals and 9 assists in 10 competitive games.

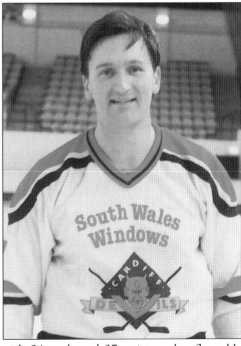

Top British scorers were Max Thurgood (left) with 24 goals and 27 assists and unflappable defenceman Paul Farmer (right) who recorded 21 and 30 in league and play-off games.

The programme cover for the Division Two championship tournament, hosted by Cardiff and featuring the three regional winners – Cardiff (Midlands), Grimsby Buffaloes (North) and Streatham Bruins (South), as well as Scottish First Division champions Aviemore Blackhawks.

Lawless scores in the 10-4 semi-final win over Grimsby. The game ended prematurely, when an attack on Lawless prompted a bench-clearing brawl involving all 34 players – 21 from Grimsby and 13 from Cardiff. Officials issued eight game misconducts, but allowed the result to stand, putting Devils through to their expected final against Aviemore.

The final face-off – referee Gordon Pirry drops the puck as John Lawless (left) clashes with Glen Campbell. Aviemore won the toss to play in their home colours, putting Cardiff in their red away strip. Blackhawks romped away to a 6-2 lead in the first period, and after a 3-3 middle session, Cardiff faced an uphill struggle in the last 20 minutes.

The final period comeback was thrilling. Here, Devils celebrate a Lawless goal which cut the lead to 9-8 with three minutes left. Just 13 seconds later Campbell extended the lead, and Cardiff could manage just one more goal – Max Thurgood making it 10-9.

Despite the disappointment of the play-offs, there was much to celebrate at the first supporters' club awards dinner. John Lawless (left) receives his player of the year award from supporters' club chairman Steve Kingdon. Having put the team together off the ice and performed magnificently on it, there was no doubt that Lawless was the deserved winner.

Glen Haley celebrates his award as most improved player of the year. The former Bradford Bulldog ended the season with 20 goals and 27 assists in the league and play-offs.

Two

Moving Up
1987-89

League restructuring meant the Devils were promoted to Division One despite their play-off defeat. The biggest new signing for the new campaign was the versatile defenceman Shannon Hope, who returned to Britain after playing with John Lawless at Peterborough two years before. He was to become one of the club's most influential players over many seasons, although this first season with Cardiff was a difficult one – he clocked up 122 penalty minutes in 22 games.

An official Devils song 'Go Devils Go' was released by South Wales folk group Cara. This picture sleeve features John Lawless and Perry Olivier, the two imports retained from the opening season. The rousing chorus ran: 'Devils away! The superfans of Cardiff say Go, Devils, Go! Devils away! From Russia to the USA, from Canada to Cardiff Bay, Go, Devils, Go, Devils away!'

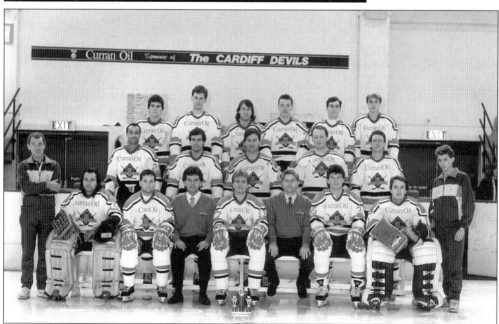

The new line-up for the Division One (South) campaign in 1987. From left to right, back row: Bleddyn Davies, Mark Garrard, Brian Dickson, Brian Wilkie, Glen Haley, Andrew Fletcher. Middle row: Robbie Morris, Paul Morganti, Paul Farmer, Steve Condren, Tim Steadman. Front row: Norm Jaques (equipment manager), Jeff Smith, John Lawless, Sean O'Neil (sponsor), Perry Olivier, Craig Burgin (sponsor), Shannon Hope, Ian Wright, Mike Jaques.

New faces: Robbie Morris (left), a speedy winger signed from Oxford City Stars. He finished the season as Cardiff's second-highest British scorer. Jeff Smith (right) arrived from Telford Tigers as first-choice netminder.

Two more new arrivals, pictured in training: Brian Dickson (right) was one of two summer signings from Aviemore, along with Brian Wilkie. Dickson was to top the club's British scorers this season. With him here is ex-Oxford man, Tim Steadman.

Another Brian arrived from Aviemore when the season had already got under way. Brian Kanewischer, a Canadian, was signed as non-playing coach. He was to finish the season under suspension after ordering his men off the ice in a hugely controversial game at Telford. (See page 25.)

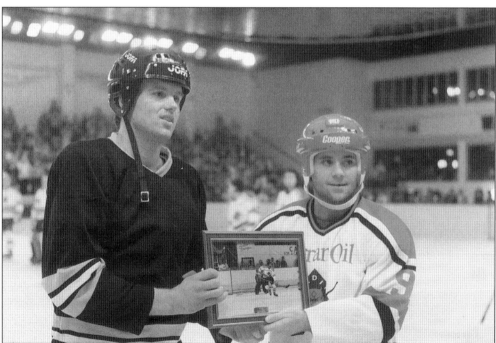

Mike Urquhart (left) brought his Chelmsford Chieftains to Cardiff for a challenge game and was awarded a memento of his Devils days, as a thank you for his contribution to the side's success in their debut season. John Lawless is pictured making the presentation.

Cardiff qualified for the Division One Autumn Trophy final against Trafford Metros. After winning the home leg 7-5, Devils travelled north for the deciding game with some 800 fans. Some of them are pictured here during a break at a motorway service station.

Left: Devils captain Perry Olivier in action during the match at Metros' Altrincham rink. Cardiff lost 5-4 on the night, giving them an 11-10 win on aggregate. *Right:* Olivier receives the congratulations for his team's first significant trophy.

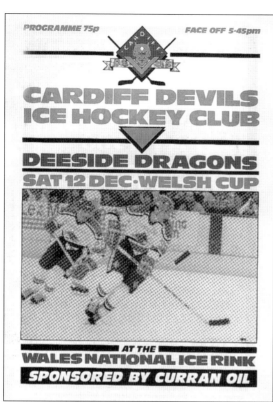

PROGRAMME 75p   FACE OFF 5-45pm

CARDIFF DEVILS
ICE HOCKEY CLUB

DEESIDE DRAGONS
SAT 12 DEC·WELSH CUP

AT THE
WALES NATIONAL ICE RINK
SPONSORED BY CURRAN OIL

More silverware came Cardiff's way with the inaugural Welsh Cup – a two-team competition, over two legs, pitting the Devils against their former Division Two rivals, now in Division One (North), Deeside Dragons. Cardiff won the home leg 6-3 and the away leg 5-2, for an aggregate 11-5 victory. The scoreline would have been greater if it had not been for the outstanding netminding of Dragons' Canadian Doug Rigby.

Perry Olivier collects the silverware at Deeside, in front of a crowd (in the spectating area on the opposite side of the rink) which included more Devils fans than locals.

Away from the cup action, Cardiff's league campaign continued solidly. Here, John Lawless approaches the net during Devils' 10-6 win over Lee Valley Lions.

John Burnicle arrived from Telford Tigers in January to boost Cardiff's defence. His debut game – a visit to his former club – proved to be one of the most controversial in British ice hockey history, and the one which led to Kanewischer's suspension. Cardiff's visit to Telford earlier in the season had left Mark Garrard sidelined for months with a fractured cheekbone and Shannon Hope banned for three games for throwing a punch. He later won an appeal, but had already served the ban. This time, Kanewischer was incensed when a series of sticking offences against his players went unpunished. When Hope received a serious injury below his eye, the coach ordered his men off the ice. He was banned for the rest of the season, and the club fined a record £1,000.

Left: Player-manager John Lawless finished the 1987/88 season as Cardiff's top scorer with 69 goals and 94 assists from 36 league and trophy games. *Right:* Lone Welshman Bleddyn Davies completed his last full season in the British game before emigrating to Australia.

Tim Steadman's shot is saved by a future Devil, Jason Wood, in the Medway Bears' goal. Cardiff pipped Medway to third place in Division One (South), behind Telford and Slough.

OLIVIER RELEASED BY DEVILS

BY ANDY WELCH

CARDIFF Devils captain Perry Olivier has been released by the club.

Player-manager John Lawless said the team would be aiming for promotion next season and needed to boost the standard of their imports.

"It came as a big shock to the ego," said Olivier. "He thought that for the money he is paying he could get a better import."

The 25-year-old from Sudbury, Ontario, was the team's second highest scorer this season with 81 goals and 79 assists in 46 games.

A founder member of the team in 1986, the talented forward was brought from Canada to help launch the Devils, and his guidance as player-coach helped the new club to promotion in their debut season.

Buy success

Now Olivier will return to Canada for the summer to consider his future.

"At the moment I don't where my future lies," he said. "It's been a bit of a shock and it's something I'll have to think about."

While his own future remains uncertain, he is confident of success for the Devils.

"I think Cardiff will w Division One next year he said. "They will p money to buy success.

"They have one of th best sponsorship dea and some of the bigge gates."

Meanwhile Lawless likely to be reclassified British next season, all wing him to sign two ne imports in addition to d fenceman Shannon Ho who is being offered a fu ther contract.

Lawless, who has British wife, will be appl ing for dual citizensh this week.

In any case, a planne rule change by the BIH will qualify him for no import status due to h period of residence.

Lawless's three-ye plan for the Devils mat res next season with t push for Premier Divisic status.

He already has son new signings in mind ar expects to be talent-spo ting at the Heinek Championships Wembley this weekend.

Left: The spring of 1988 brought the news that captain Perry Olivier was being released to make way for a top quality import to lead Cardiff's push for promotion to the Heineken Premier Division. *Right:* The man who replaced him was Steve Moria, stepping down to Division One after a season and a half with Premier Division Fife Flyers, with whom he had been the top scorer in the play-offs.

Even more audacious was the signing of brothers Stephen (left) and Ian Cooper from mighty Durham Wasps, the Heineken play-off champions. The Great Britain internationals were two of the top home-grown players in the game and their move to Cardiff on two-year contracts shocked the sport's establishment and led to protests of 'cheque book hockey'.

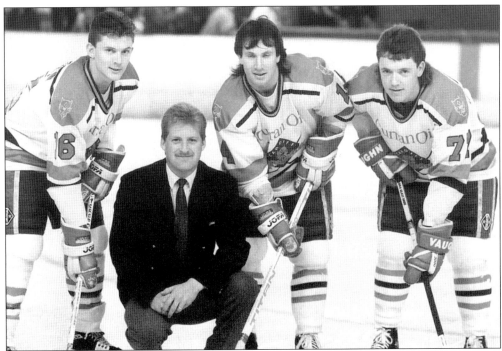

Another new arrival for the 1988/89 campaign was Archie Nelson (left), completing a quartet of defectors from Aviemore – with Brian Kanewischer, Brian Dickson and Brian Wilkie.

The 1988/89 squad assembled to make the big push for the top flight. From left to right, back row: Bleddyn Davies, Robbie Morris, Tim Steadman, Brian Wilkie, John Burnicle. Middle row: Brian Dickson, Stephen Cooper, Mark Garrard, Ian Cooper, Andrew Fletcher, Archie Nelson. Front row: Jeff Smith, John Lawless, Craig Burgin (sponsor), Steve Moria, Brian Kanewischer (coach), Shannon Hope, Ian Wright.

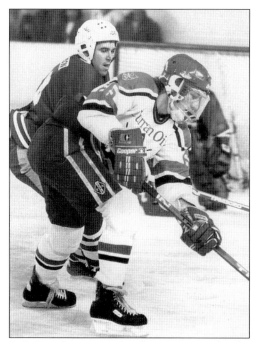

Left: Ian Cooper made a huge impact, finishing the season as Cardiff's top British scorer with 64 goals and 48 assists in his 24 league games. His highly physical style of play also earned him 113 penalty minutes, making him the most penalised player in Division One. *Right:* His older brother, Stephen, was equally influential. Despite being a defenceman, he was the club's second highest British scorer, and helped ensure Devils lost only two league games.

Steve Moria was the club's top scorer with 85 goals and 93 assists in 24 league games. Only Luc Chabot of Medway Bears bettered him in the division. Here, Moria scores in an international challenge match against touring Canadian Junior B side St Albert's Merchants, which finished 8-8.

Mark Garrard left Cardiff mid-season because he was unhappy with his lack of ice-time. His departure, which followed those of Bleddyn Davies and Tim Steadman for similar reasons, left Lawless as the only original Devil.

Shannon Hope remained a central component of the team, as Cardiff beat Medway to retain the Autumn Trophy and then pipped the Bears in the chase for the Division One title. The only title lost in the season was the Welsh Cup against Deeside, which saw Cardiff coast to a 24-6 win in the home leg before sending a B side to Clwyd for the decider, which Dragons won 32-0. Hope and most of the Devils team remained in Cardiff to play for a select team against the Great Britain Under 21s.

Steve Moria scores a penalty shot at Telford to help Devils to an 11-4 win, which clinched the Division One title. Five hundred Cardiff fans made the trip – a phenomenal figure for a midweek game.

Left: Brian Dickson climbs the plexiglass to celebrate with fans. *Right:* Player-manager John Lawless and coach Brian Kanewischer (right) get their hands on the Division One trophy.

Devils had to overcome the Premier Division's bottom side, Streatham Redskins, in home and away play-offs to gain promotion. Here, Lawless scores one of his five goals in Cardiff's 12-1 win in the home leg.

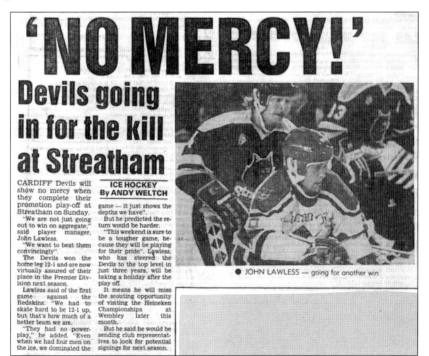

'NO MERCY!'
Devils going in for the kill at Streatham

CARDIFF Devils will show no mercy when they complete their promotion play-off at Streatham on Sunday.

"We are not just going out to win on aggregate," said player manager, John Lawless.

"We want to beat them convincingly".

The Devils won the home leg 12-1 and are now virtually assured of their place in the Premier Division next season.

Lawless said of the first game against the Redskins: "We had to skate hard to be 12-1 up, but that's how much of a better team we are.

"They had no power-play," he added. "Even when we had four men on the ice, we dominated the

ICE HOCKEY
By ANDY WELTCH

game — it just shows the depths we have".

But he predicted the return would be harder.

"This weekend is sure to be a tougher game, because they will be playing for their pride". Lawless, who has steered the Devils to the top level in just three years, will be taking a holiday after the play off.

It means he will miss the scouting opportunity of visiting the Heineken Championships at Wembley later this month.

But he said he would be sending club representatives to look for potential signings for next season.

● JOHN LAWLESS — going for another win

After dominating the first game, Cardiff promised no mercy when they visited the home of the famous London club for the return. Devils won 9-5 to secure their place in the Premier Division. Cardiff's successful season was underlined with Devils players Jeff Smith, Stephen Cooper, Shannon Hope and Steve Moria filling four of the six places in the Division One All-Star team, which was voted for by journalists.

Three
Against the Odds
1989-90

With player-manager John Lawless obtaining his British passport in the summer of 1989, he filled the vacant import slot with Doug McEwen, who had led Lee Valley Lions to an unexpected win over Cardiff the previous season. McEwen is pictured (centre), as Peterborough Pirates' Todd Bidner fires a slapshot past Shannon Hope.

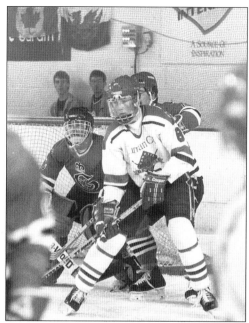

Veteran defenceman Paul Farmer (left) returned after a year away, while young Nicky Chinn (right), a product of Cardiff's junior programme, got an early taste of life in the top flight. He is pictured during a challenge match against touring Canadian veterans King George Old-Timers.

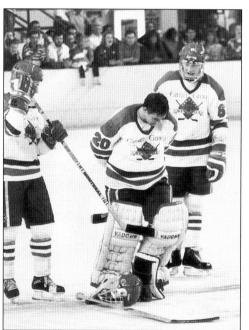

Chris Newton (left) arrived from Peterborough as a new back-up netminder, but later returned to the Pirates and was replaced by Jason Wood. He is seen reluctantly moving forward to collect the man of the match award after a 13-2 challenge match victory over Swindon Wildcats. Paul Cousins (right), a regular with the Under 21 Cardiff Satans, made his home Devils debut against Ayr Raiders in November.

Murrayfield Racers emerged as Devils' chief rivals in Cardiff's first Premier season. Brian Dickson (right) with fellow Scot, Racers' star forward Tony Hand. Dickson would later leave the club and was killed in a road accident in Australia in July 1995. His number 14 shirt was retired at the start of the 1995/96 season.

Half-way through the 1989/90 season, Cardiff's achievements of the previous three years were rewarded with *The Western Mail*'s team of the year title at the newspaper's awards night.

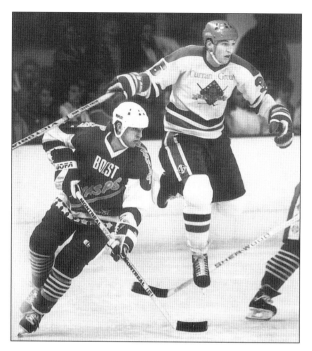

Shannon Hope, a professional pilot in Canada, takes off over Stephen Johnson's stick during a clash with Durham. Cardiff beat the English giants twice home and twice away during the season, including a 10-0 scoreline, which marked the first Premier shut-out in two years, the first ever inflicted on Durham, and the heaviest defeat ever suffered by Wasps. There was revenge in the Norwich Union Autumn Cup, however, when Durham beat Cardiff in the 'English' final.

Fife Flyers were another big-name club with a long history (founded 1938) who were shown precious little respect by the newly-promoted Welsh club. Here, John Burnicle (right) closes in on Les Millie in a match Cardiff won 12-4.

Having been classed as 'English' for the purposes of the Norwich Union Cup, Devils were invited to be 'Scottish' to make up the numbers for the Capital Foods Scottish Cup, following the withdrawal of Tayside Tigers. Here, some of Cardiff's fans take a break on their way to the tournament.

Steve Moria, seen here discussing a point of law with linesman Simon Kirkham, was badly injured in the Scottish Cup semi-final against Ayr Raiders, and Devils lost the final to Murrayfield 13-4.

John Lawless, determined as ever, helped his team to a sensational success in the Premier Division, clinching the league title against all predictions and bookmakers' odds of 100-1.

With Steve Moria injured, Lawless as acting captain collected the Heineken League trophy when Murrayfield were the visitors on 16 March for a televised BBC *Grandstand* programme.

As a British citizen, Lawless got the call up for Great Britain. Here, he faces Swiss club Davos – featuring his second cousin Paul Lawless – in a challenge match at Nottingham.

Cardiff was chosen to host Pool D of the world championships, featuring Spain and Australia. Great Britain comfortably won the tournament, and promotion to Pool C, with a squad which included Jeff Smith, Stephen and Ian Cooper, as well as Lawless. Stephen Cooper was named defenceman of the tournament.

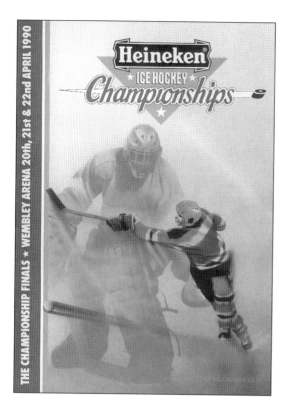

Devils topped their three-team play-off group to book a place at the sport's showpiece, the Heineken Championships weekend at Wembley. They beat Fife 5-1 in Friday night's semi-final to face league runners-up Murrayfield in the final on Sunday. In front of a live national television audience, Racers – in their fifth Wembley final in seven years – skated off to a 3-0 lead after 16 minutes, but Cardiff fought back and a Stephen Cooper goal two minutes from time made it 6-6. With no score in overtime, the game went into a penalty shoot-out.

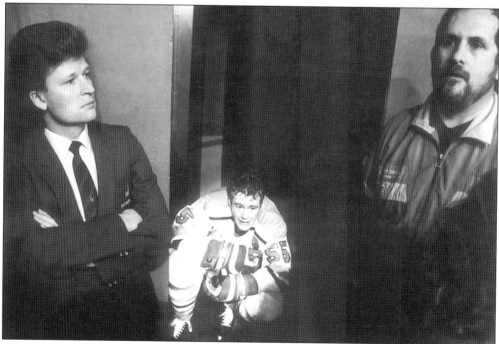

The tension was almost tangible, even to those watching at home. After missing two penalties, Stephen Cooper could not watch the rest of the shoot-out, but crouched in the tunnel and prayed.

40

Steve Moria scores Cardiff's third penalty to put the Devils in the driving seat. The BBC delayed their snooker coverage in order to show viewers the thrilling climax of hockey's big weekend.

Tony Hand's shot is blocked by Jeff Smith. Hand was to miss all three of his efforts, the last of them giving the Welsh side the championship.

Play-off beards and the sponsor's lager are much in evidence, as Cardiff celebrate a sensational conclusion to their first season in the Premier Division.

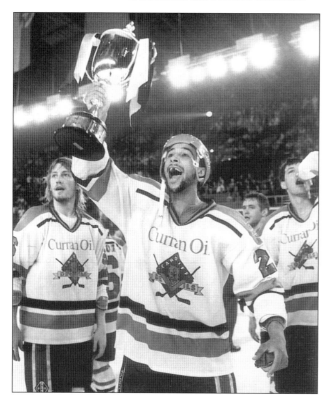

Robbie Morris holds the trophy aloft. The Wembley final was to be his last game for Cardiff.

Mission accomplished – Lawless gets his hands on the British game's most prestigious trophy, in a moment he had aimed for since launching the club less than four years earlier.

Left: The Coopers had been here before with Durham, but never had the final been won in such dramatic fashion. *Right:* After the tension and the celebrations, Robbie Morris and Brian Wilkie are exhausted on the coach trip home.

Devils' success made them the talk of the South Wales sports scene. This cartoon by Gren in the *South Wales Echo* shows how the team's achievements dwarfed those of Cardiff's cricket, rugby and soccer clubs.

It was hard to choose individuals from such a successful season, but the supporters club voted Doug McEwen (left) player of the year and Jeff Smith (right) British player of the year. The British Ice Hockey Writers Association named Smith, Stephen Cooper, Shannon Hope and Steve Moria in their Premier Division All-Star team, with Moria player of the year, Brian Kanewischer coach of the year, and Stephen Cooper recipient of the Alan Weeks Trophy as best British defenceman.

Four
Life at the Top
1990-96

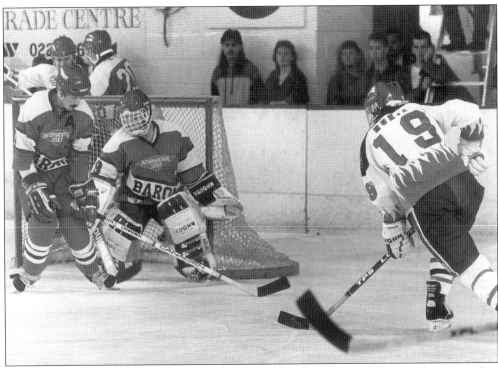

As champions, Cardiff became the team to beat, and without the Coopers, who returned to Durham in the summer, and coach Kanewischer, who had moved to Ayr, Devils were less of a force. Solihull managed one win in the teams' four encounters in 1990/91. Here, Steve Moria fires in a hopeful shot in a home game in October.

Two new signings from Peterborough Pirates were Scottish enforcer Paul Heavey (on the right-hand side of the picture) and hard-checking winger Peter Smith. Heavey in particular was signed to give Devils a more physical presence. He is pictured here in the Norwich Union Cup match against Whitley Bay Warriors, which Cardiff won 9-6. Devils reached the semi-final, which they lost to Durham Wasps.

Peter Smith proved a useful addition to the attack, finishing the season as the team's second-highest British scorer. He is pictured during a 5-9 home defeat by Durham. In eight encounters with Wasps in league, cup and challenges in 1990/91, Cardiff won just once.

Another new face was Neil Browne, signed from Slough Jets, who was to be Devils' top British scorer in 1990/91. In 32 league games, he scored 20 goals and 32 assists, with just six penalty minutes.

The twenty-year-old Derek King arrived from Fife Flyers to bolster the defence. His transfer fee of £6,900 set a club record.

The 1990/91 squad. From left to right, back row: Derek King, Neil Browne, Brian Wilkie, Archie Nelson, John Burnicle. Middle row: Owen Jenkins (equipment manager), Peter Smith, Nicky Chinn, Paul Heavey, Jason Stone, Jason Ellery (equipment). Front row: Jeff Smith, Shannon Hope, Steve Moria, Paul Farmer (coach), John Lawless, Doug McEwen, Jason Wood. Captain Moria and player-manager Lawless shared the coaching duties at the start of the season, before Farmer was persuaded to take up the coaching role – only to be released at the end of January.

John Burnicle wore the 'A' for assistant captain with pride. Always a tenacious and hard-working defenceman, he is pictured preparing to fire the puck towards goal in a league match against Whitley Bay.

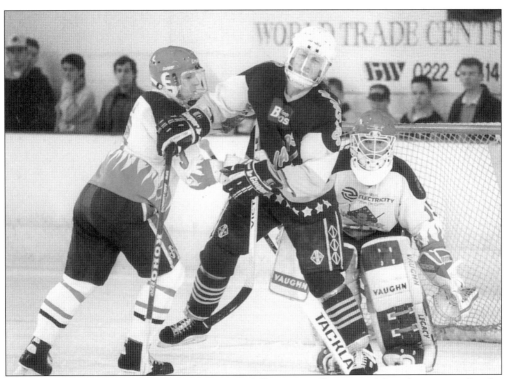

Durham and Ian Cooper's return visits to Cardiff were usually successful in this season, but he didn't get an easy ride. Here, Derek King tries to keep him away from Jeff Smith's goal.

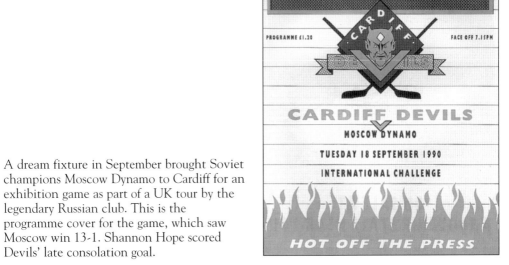

A dream fixture in September brought Soviet champions Moscow Dynamo to Cardiff for an exhibition game as part of a UK tour by the legendary Russian club. This is the programme cover for the game, which saw Moscow win 13-1. Shannon Hope scored Devils' late consolation goal.

As the previous season's league champions, Cardiff qualified for the European Cup quarter-final tournament in Copenhagen. This is the programme cover for the tournament, which featured the champions of Norway and Poland, as well as Cardiff and the Danish hosts.

Devils fans celebrate an amazing scoreline in the opening game, which saw unfancied Cardiff beat Danish hosts Rodovre.

The result prompted predictions that Cardiff could win the group and become the first British side to reach the European semi-finals, but lack of manpower proved their downfall, and leads in their other two matches were lost in the last period. There was plenty to celebrate, however – (below) players from both teams seem stunned after the match, as a young Welsh fan flies the flag.

DEVILS JOY IN EUROPE!

CARDIFF Devils were today being tipped as possible winners of their European Cup quarter-final group, after a sensational 11-8 win over hosts Rodovre here last night.

The result left Scandinavian journalists predicting a

ICE HOCKEY
From Andy Welch in Copenhagen

showdown for the semi-final place between the Devils and Polish champions Polonia, who beat favourites Furuset of Norway 3-0 yesterday.

Cardiff's victory was the best result ever achieved by a British club in Europe, and coach Paul Farmer admitted he was "shaken" by the outcome.

"The most we thought we could get against those lads was a draw," he said.

"We never expected to go out and beat them, but the team played their heart and soul out.

"It could have gone either way, but we just jumped on them, and jumped on them hard.

"We were the underdogs here, but now we've proved to everybody that they've got to take us seriously."

After Cardiff's dazzling display, which included a burst of three goals in just 25 seconds, the Norwegians were reported to be nervous about facing the British champions later today.

Before the tournament, Furuset were favourites and Cardiff complete outsiders.

And despite the euphoria after last night's win, Devils' player-manager John Lawless warned

the remaining games would be much tougher.

"Both the Polish and Norwegians are much stronger in defence," he said.

"Polonia have the Olympic team goalie and Canada only scored one goal against him."

Derek King put Cardiff ahead in the third minute, but the Danes quickly equalised, and took the lead midway through the first period.

"The Danes were really pretty weak on defence – I had four or five breakaways."

The game then followed a pattern of Cardiff equalising and Rodovre going ahead again — but only by one goal.

But Cardiff hit back with an incredible three goals in 25 seconds to take a 7-4 lead with five minutes of the middle season left.

Shannon Hope, who spent virtually the whole game on the ice, Brian Wilkie and Lawless were the men who got those crucial goals in a match which saw the scoring shared.

● HARD WORKER — *Shannon Hope stayed on the ice for most of last night's historic Devils victory*

Devils v Furuset: Report in Football Echo, tonight

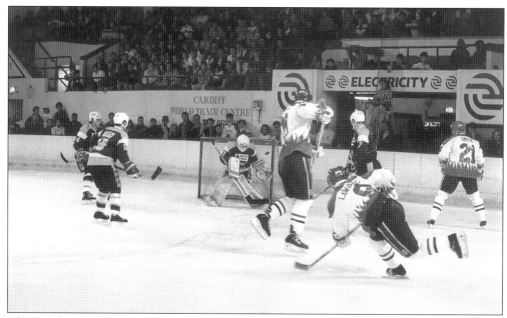

Above: John Lawless fires home a goal past Whitley Bay Warriors. *Below:* top scorer Steve Moria (left) and Nicky Chinn celebrate a goal against Murrayfield Racers. Chinn was named young British player of the year in a season which saw Cardiff finish second in the league and lose to Peterborough in the Wembley semi-finals.

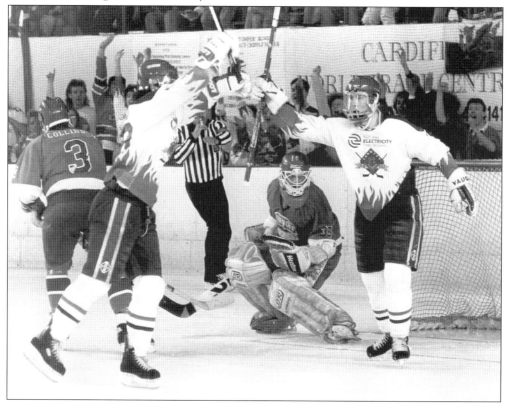

As young British player of the year, Chinn joined the National Hockey League's Calgary Flames for their pre-season training, which meant he missed most of Cardiff's Autumn Cup matches. Devils again exited the competition at the semi-final stage, losing to eventual winners Nottingham Panthers.

The new season brought a new coach in John Griffith, a Dutch-Canadian with Welsh ancestry and an impressive record in Holland, despite a disappointing earlier spell at Peterborough in his only previous British appointment. Here he is seen (left) signing his contract, with player-manager John Lawless.

September 1991 saw the visit of SKA Leningrad for a highly entertaining international challenge. The Russians won 9-4, but the game saw Cardiff use a full squad, including many youngsters. *Left:* Derek King remains cool under pressure. *Below:* Robert Hill was one of the young Welsh players given the chance to face Leningrad.

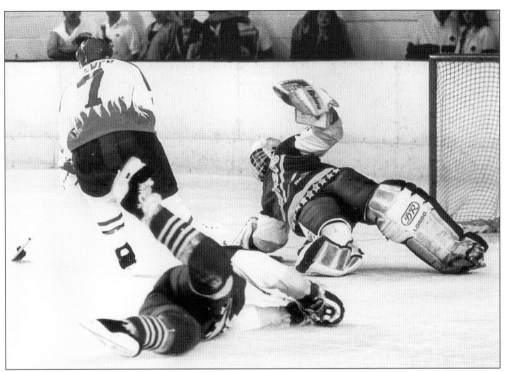

Doug McEwen leaves Durham Wasps' defence stranded on Cardiff's way to a 5-2 challenge win. Devils were less successful in league clashes with the Wasps, however, winning just one of the four games.

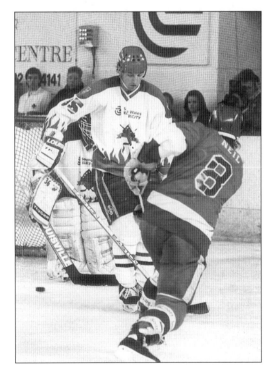

Shannon Hope tries to shield netminder Jeff Smith from a Scott Neil shot in a match against Murrayfield Racers. Hope was in trouble in November, when a fight with Nottingham's Chris Kelland during the post-match handshakes led to an eleven-game suspension, later reduced to six.

Netminder Jeff Smith and local prodigy Nicky Chinn were called into the Great Britain squad, along with Devils player-manager John Lawless, for a trial match against Denmark, as part of the build-up to the Pool C world championship. Great Britain won this game at Basingstoke 3-2. In the end, Hope was the only Devil in the championship squad.

Durham's visit on 5 January 1992 marked a low point in Cardiff's history. Here, Devils' Neil Browne (left) and Peter Smith leave Wasps' John Hutley on the boards. The game saw the visitors skate to a 13-0 win, marking Devils' first shut-out, their heaviest defeat and their fourth successive loss on home ice. Although no single player could be blamed for such a lacklustre performance, it was no surprise when Jeff Smith was dropped from the squad.

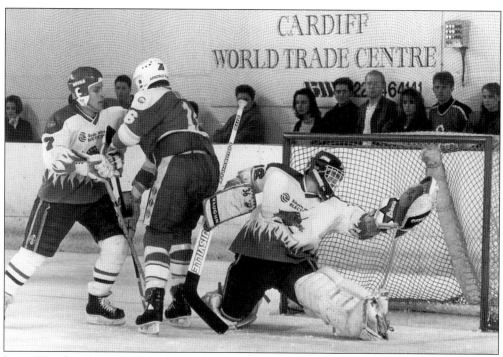

Jason Wood took over as first choice between the pipes. Here, he pulls off a glove save against Billingham Bombers in the last Heineken League game of the season. Devils won 10-5, but finished only third in the Premier Division.

John Lawless continued to lead by example, but he described the 1991/92 campaign as 'disappointing and inconsistent'. The league finish was poor by Cardiff's high standards, but worse was failing to reach the Wembley play-off finals. The team lost 8-4 away to Whitley Bay Warriors in front of BBC's *Grandstand* cameras.

There was a break in league action, when a first-ever Wales Select team faced Romania in February. The Select team was a cosmopolitan line-up of Cardiff players with a few guests. Sadly, the opportunity of creating a more representative Welsh side by including players from Deeside Dragons (at this time playing in the non-import English Conference) was missed, but Wales won 9-3.

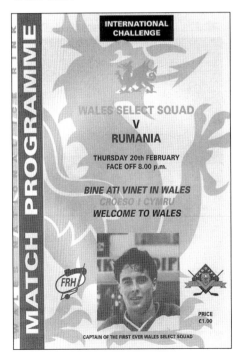

Wales Select team *v.* Romania programme, featuring captain Steve Moria on the cover.

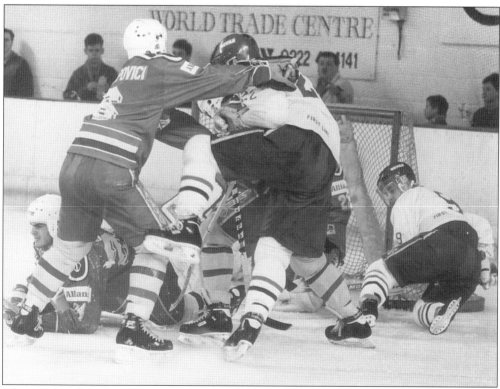

John Lawless (right) is knocked to the ice during a scramble in front of the Romanian net.

New faces and familiar faces at the pre-season media launch for 1992/93. From left to right: young Canadian imports Trent Andison and Brad Gratton with Ian and Stephen Cooper, who returned from Durham. The new import slots were opened up by Doug McEwen and Shannon Hope being reclassified as British, while Steve Moria had left for a player-coach role at English League Blackburn Hawks. Lawless had replaced John Griffiths as non-playing coach, while Neil Browne, Peter Smith and Jeff Smith had all moved on.

The new Canadians – Gratton is seen here in face-off with Slouth Jets captain Gary Stefan – made disappointing starts and both were soon playing elsewhere. Lawless donned his skates again before finding suitable replacements.

The new imports were Hilton Ruggles, seen above (right) moving in on Murrayfield Racers' Tony Hand, and a newcomer to Britain, Steve Cadieux (below). Their arrival sparked a winning streak of 14 games which put Cardiff two points clear at the top of the Heineken Premier Division, with three games in hand. Ruggles was Devils' top scorer, with 100 goals and 78 assists in 45 league, play-off and cup games.

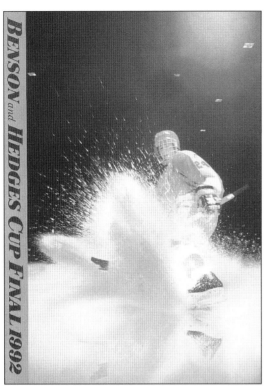

BENSON and HEDGES CUP FINAL 1992

Cardiff reached their first Autumn Cup final, now under the sponsorship of Benson & Hedges, and beat Whitley Bay Warriors 10-4 at Sheffield to win Devils' first major trophy for two and half years.

Nicky Chinn, pictured front centre of the celebrating group netted a hat-trick and took the man of the match award.

If Sheffield Arena had been a great occasion, Wembley was even better. Cardiff reached the 1993 Heineken Championships without dropping a point in their play-off group, and crushed Murrayfield 9-0 in the Friday night semi-final – Jason Wood became the first netminder to record a Wembley shut-out. Sunday's final, against outsiders Humberside Seahawks, saw a 7-4 win for Cardiff, completing the Grand Slam of league, cup and play-offs.

The programme cover for the 1993 Wembley championships – a weekend which saw Cardiff score 16 goals and concede just four.

Captain Paul Heavey collects the final Heineken Championship trophy. The win made Cardiff only the third team to complete the modern era Grand Slam, after Dundee Rockets in 1983/84 and Durham Wasps in 1990/91.

John Lawless had reason to be happy. After his early season import worries, his team had won the league by a record 16 points on their way to the Grand Slam treble. Four of his team – the Cooper brothers, Shannon Hope and Doug McEwen – had also been key figures in the British national team's victory in Pool B of the world championship, earning promotion to the top flight for the first time since 1962. Stephen Cooper and Hilton Ruggles were named in the All-Star team, with Cooper again Best British Defenceman and Lawless himself coach of the year.

With Steve Cadieux returning overseas, Devils replaced him with one of the best centremen in the British game – Durham's twenty-nine-year-old top scorer, Rick Brebant. Pictured here, left, with Ian Cooper, Brebant finished the season as Cardiff's top scorer, and third among the Premier Division hitmen. His linemate Cooper suffered a knee injury in an ill-tempered Charity Shield game with Durham in August 1993, which interrupted his season and led to the Englishman temporarily taking over the coaching duties, while Lawless again filled in on the ice. Brebant and Cooper are seen here against Fife Flyers, who enjoyed a highly successful season, inspired by new arrival Doug Smail (right of picture) who had arrived after 13 seasons in the National Hockey League. Another new name at Fife was Derek King – Devils' second summer departure.

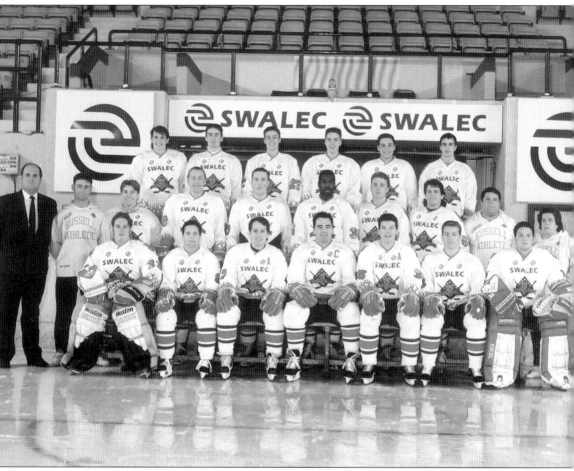

Cardiff's 1993/94 line-up. From left to right, back row: Neil Francis, Richard Townsend, Simon Keating, James Manson, Lee Carson, Gareth Owen. Middle row: Owen Jenkins (assistant manager), Jason Ellery (equipment), Jon-Paul Guy, Ian Cooper, Nicky Chinn, Hilton Ruggles, Jason Stone, Rick Brebant, John Marshall (equipment), Heather Prew (physiotherapist). Front row: Sean Ward, John Lawless, Doug McEwen, Paul Heavey, Shannon Hope, Stephen Cooper, Jason Wood.

This was the squad which secured the British League title by a record 22 points, recording 18 games without defeat on the way – a run which ended in decisive fashion with a 12-2 loss at Fife Flyers in February 1994.

A 6-2 defeat by Murrayfield Racers in the Benson & Hedges Cup final at Sheffield Arena in December 1993 ended any hopes of another Grand Slam. In the European Cup, Devils went to Latvia, where the anticipated defeats by Sokol Kiev and Riga were followed by victory over Lithuanian champions Vilnius to take third place in the quarter-final group. Hilton Ruggles was the tournament's top scorer.

The end of April 1994 saw the play-off finals at Wembley, and a 9-5 semi-final win over Fife before facing Sheffield in the final. Hilton Ruggles and Ian Cooper combine to score one of 12 past Steelers' goaltender Martin McKay.

Nicky Chinn is swamped by team-mates congratulating him on a record four goals in a Wembley final.

For John Lawless (left) this was becoming something of a habit. For the team (above), another league and championship double was worth celebrating, but it was to be Cardiff's last Wembley victory.

Shannon Hope sets off on a high-speed lap of honour to mark the big Wembley win. Figures produced by club statistician Owen Jenkins at the end of the 1993/94 season showed Hope had played more games for Cardiff than any other player – 396 matches. He also held the record for penalty minutes, with a total of 988.

Facing the press – Hilton Ruggles and John Lawless get serious for the post-match media conference. Lawless was again coach of the year, Stephen Cooper the best British defenceman and he and Brebant were both named in the writers' all-star team.

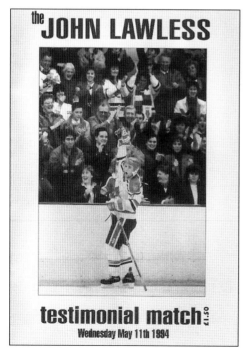

the **JOHN LAWLESS**

testimonial match £1.50
Wednesday May 11th 1994

The club was one of several in trouble with the British Ice Hockey Association for breaking the wage cap in 1993/94, but the season ended on a light note with a testimonial game for Lawless, who announced he was hanging up his skates (again!)

Brebant's departure in the summer of 1994 left an opening for another Canadian forward, Claude Dumas, to play in Devils' colours. Dumas had spent three years with Whitley Warriors before starting the 1993/94 season with Sheffield Steelers and ending it with Division One side Trafford Metros, where he had netted 105 goals in 30 league games. He went on to register 65 goals in his 43 Premier Division games for Cardiff, as Devils' second-highest goal-scorer of the season.

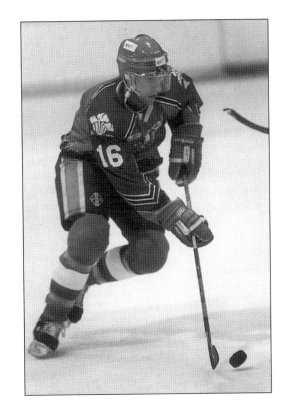

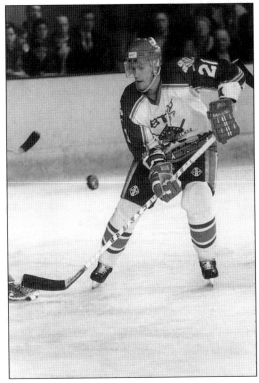

Another new name on the team sheet for 1994/95 was the much-travelled Peter Smith. Since leaving the Devils two years before, he had appeared for Swindon Wildcats, Milton Keynes Kings and Slough Jets.

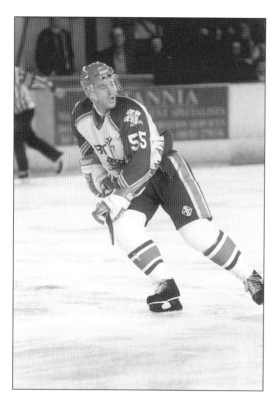

Ace British defenceman Stephen Cooper missed a large part of the season with a knee injury and, with Paul Heavey suffering an injury that would force him into early retirement, the team had to call on some of its forwards to help out at the back. His absence meant Cooper even missed out on the British defenceman of the year award.

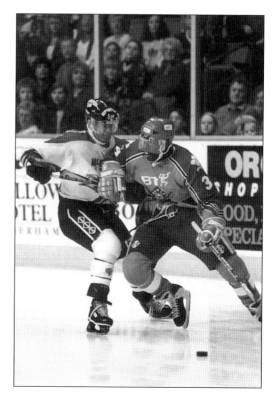

Hilton Ruggles, seen here in hard-checking action against Sheffield Steelers, was Devils' top scorer for 1994/95 with 136 goals and 84 assists in 64 league, cup, and play-off games.

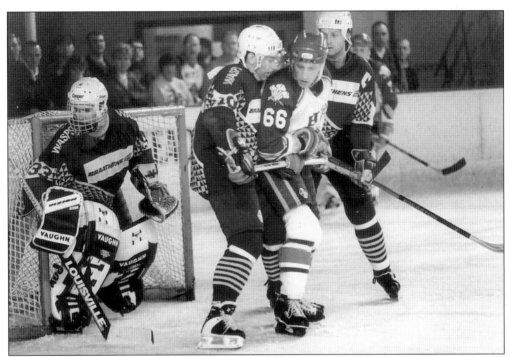

Ian Cooper was again Cardiff's top British scorer. Here, he causes trouble for the defence of his former team Durham. Honours were shared in the league this season, with both teams winning their two home games against each other. Cardiff had the better of their old rivals in the play-offs, however – with a 4-4 tie at Durham and a 13-1 win at home, and in the Benson & Hedges Cup, where Devils won both quarter-final legs 4-3 away and 15-2 at home.

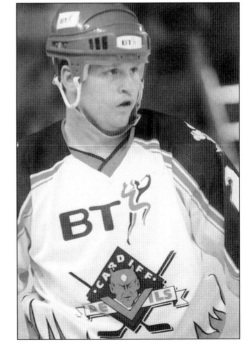

Specialist defenceman Jamie van der Horst arrived just before Cardiff's unsuccessful Benson & Hedges final, which saw a 7-2 defeat by Nottingham Panthers at Sheffield Arena. The Dutch-Canadian proved a popular and valuable addition to Devils' blue line.

Young Welsh winger Nicky Chinn soon got used to the physical side of the game, and finished the 1994/95 season as Devils' most penalised player. Here, he clashes with Slough Jets veteran Gary Stefan in a Benson & Hedges group game, which Cardiff won 6-3.

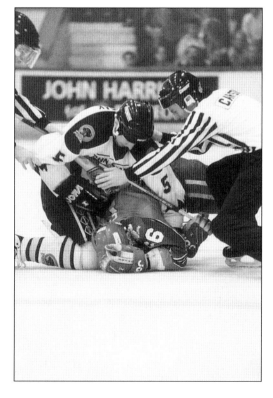

Ian Cooper was no stranger to the rough stuff either. Here he covers up after an altercation during a game at Nottingham Panthers.

Cardiff's third venture into the European Cup was nothing short of sensational. They beat the champions of Kazakhstan and Ukraine to win the quarter-final group in Holland and reach the semis. Young netminder Stevie Lyle, aged just fourteen, was the star of the tournament. *Above:* Lyle prepares for a shot from a Sokol Kiev forward. *Below:* Another Welshman, Nicky Chinn, skates away after beating Vladimir Borodulin in the Torpedo Ust Kamenogorsk goal.

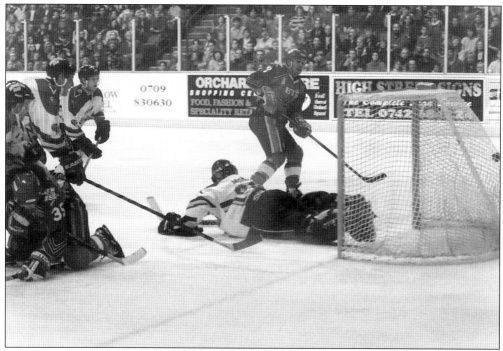

Doug McEwen leaves Sheffield netminder Martin McKay stranded as he scores one of his 63 league goals in this season. The tally was all the more impressive in light of the fact that the versatile McEwen spent much of the season filling in on defence. In March, Sheffield ended Cardiff's unbeaten home run of 50 games, and went on to defeat them in Devils' last Wembley appearance – a semi-final Steelers win on penalty shots following a 4-4 scoreline after overtime.

Jason Wood found his place as Devils' first-choice goaltender under threat after Stevie Lyle's success in Europe. Still only fifteen at the end of the season, Lyle finished second in the Premier Division standings.

Two of the hottest new talents to emerge in a season which saw Devils without any major silverware, were Richard Townsend (left) and Stevie Lyle (right edge of picture). Townsend, aged eighteen, finished the season as Cardiff's sixth highest British scorer in the league, while Lyle was the Premier Division's second-top netminder with an average 4.13 goals-against per game.

Another product of the Cardiff junior development programme, Jason Stone, came into his own following a move to defence, forced by injuries to more established players. The unassuming twenty-two-year-old helped Cardiff to runners-up spot in the Premier Division, and was called up to the Great Britain training camp as a result.

Departures in the summer of 1995 included John Lawless, who went as manager and coach to the newly-formed Manchester Storm in Division One, Hilton Ruggles, Claude Dumas, and Cardiff-trained Nicky Chinn, James Manson and Lee Carson. Among the more significant arrivals was Canadian hard man Mike Ware, a twenty-eight-year-old defenceman who had spent the past three years with Murrayfield Racers. He became one of the Premier Division's most penalised players, with 169 minutes in 32 league games.

Ware was united with older brother Greg, whose three years in Britain had been spent in Division One, with Slough, Dumfries and Trafford.

Randy Smith arrived from Peterborough Pirates to lead the attack, and he became the division's third highest scorer, with 51 goals and 49 assists in his 36 league games, and a further 26 goals and 21 assists in play-off and Benson & Hedges Cup matches. He was the only Devil in the end-of-season All-Star team.

Another new man up front was Slovakian-born Ivan Matulik, a former team-mate of Mike Ware at Murrayfield, having previously played for Sheffield. Matulik was Devils' fourth highest scorer of the season.

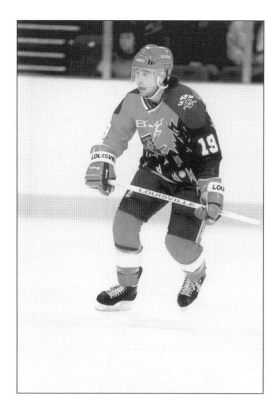

Steve Moria made a welcome return after his two-year exile, which had taken him to Division One side Blackburn and Swindon. Moria immediately settled back into the demands of Premier Division hockey, and finished second in the club-scoring chart behind Smith.

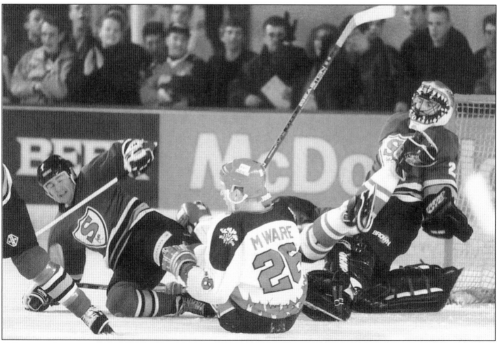

When Mike Ware switched from defence to the wing in December 1995, his move sparked an 18-game unbeaten run. Here, he causes chaos in front of the goal of newly-promoted Slough Jets. Cardiff's only shut-out of the league campaign was a 12-0 home win over Slough in January 1996.

The New Year arrival of NHL veteran Doug Smail was a further boost. The thirty-eight-year-old Smail had played in Devils colours during their European Cup semi-final tournament the previous season.

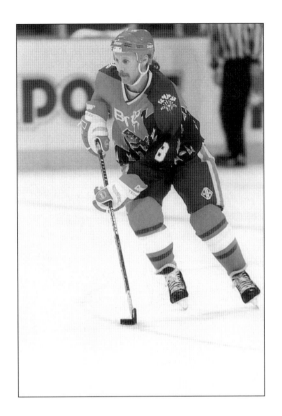

A less astute signing by the Premier Division's coach of the year Paul Heavey was Frenchman Robert Millette, who arrived just before the transfer deadline, replacing local youngster Simon Keating, whose release did not please fans. Millette's form – 4 goals and 5 assists in 15 games – was not impressive.

Ian Cooper (number 66) and Steve Moria are pictured engaged in goalmouth action against Newcastle (formerly Whitley) Warriors, despite the attentions of defenceman Terry Ord. Cardiff beat Newcastle in five of their six league and play-off encounters. The other game was a 3-3 tie at Newcastle in January.

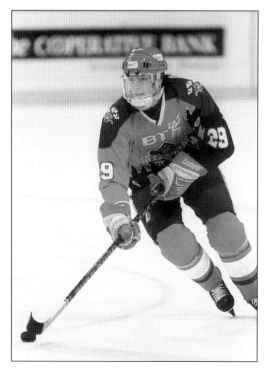

Twenty-year-old Cardiff product Neil Francis grew in confidence as the season wore on, notching up his 100th appearance in a Devils shirt.

Goaltending phenomenon Stevie Lyle again finished second in the league standings, this time with an average 3.62 goals-against, at the age of just sixteen. In April 1996 he became the youngest player ever capped by Great Britain, backstopping the national team to a notable 4-2 win over Belarus in the world championships.

Great Britain's captain Shannon Hope enjoyed his best season for many years and played his 500th game for Cardiff. He led Great Britain to second place in the Olympic qualifying tournament and fourth in Pool B of the world championships.

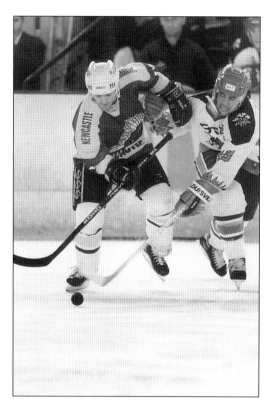

Despite reaching second place in the final British League Premier Division, Cardiff struggled in the play-offs. Newcastle were the only team they beat twice. Here, a determined Steve Moria chases the puck against the Warriors.

Durham Wasps caused Cardiff the most difficulty in the final Premier Division play-offs, winning their home and away legs. Durham, now owned by Newcastle United Sporting Club, were playing temporarily out of Sunderland's small Crowtree rink, pending their move to replace the Warriors in Newcastle. Ex-Devil Rick Brebant was back in their line-up as player-coach and topped the club's scoring. Here, Devils' Doug McEwen tries to halt his progress.

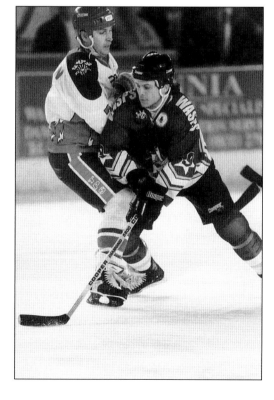

Five

Superleague
1996-99

The arrival of the all-professional Superleague led to a flurry of North American signings by the eight clubs who made up the new competition. None was more impressive than thirty-six-year-old millionaire Glenn Anderson, whose on-off negotiations with Cardiff ended after a single appearance in a pre-season game against Stuttgart. Anderson scored the opening goal in a 6-1 win, but talks foundered over money – Devils claimed he was asking for £7,000 a week. Anderson had played 16 NHL seasons, scored almost 600 goals in league and play-off games, and skated alongside all-time greats Wayne Gretzky and Mark Messier in Edmonton Oilers' Stanley Cup winning team. His arrival at the Cardiff rink was appropriately flamboyant – here he steps out of a limousine, which was driven onto the ice.

With Stevie Lyle spending the start of the season in North America with Detroit Whalers, Devils coach Paul Heavey signed up ex-NHL netminder Frank Caprice (pictured), a veteran of 100 NHL games over six seasons. Caprice was a quality goaltender by any measure, yet when Lyle returned – a victim of North American restrictions on foreign players – the Canadian found himself playing second fiddle. Lyle topped the league's averages with 2.78 goals per game and was named Superleague's first player of the year.

The defence was bolstered by the arrival of Brent Pope (pictured) from the American Hockey League, Kip Noble from Durham Wasps (now transformed into Newcastle Cobras for the Superleague) and Frank Evans from Fife Flyers. Pope ended the season as one of the league's most penalised players.

In attack, Doug McCarthy proved a valuable acquisition, having spent five seasons with Milton Keynes Kings. The Canadian, whose summers were spent as one of North America's top roller hockey stars, finished the season as Cardiff's second highest scorer, and years later would move into management at the club.

Another new arrival, George Swan, made less of an impact and was released before the end of the season. His signing was an example of what became a trend in Superleague, with clubs preferring to sign Canadians over Britons and not always ensuring that they were of the calibre required.

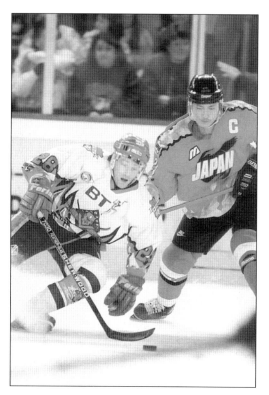

Nobody questioned the wisdom of bringing Italian-Canadian Vezio Sacratini to Wales. The diminutive Italian international showed all the tenacity and agility Devils fans had seen from John Lawless ten years before. He topped the club's scoring with 29 goals and 50 assists in 54 league, play-off and Benson & Hedges Cup games. He is pictured here in a challenge match against Japan in February 1997, which the tourists won 5-3.

Another Canadian newcomer was Marty Yewchuk, pictured in the same match. Yewchuk hit the headlines in October 1996 when he swung his stick onto the head of Nottingham Panthers' Daryl Olsen in retaliation for an elbow to the head. The incident, seen on Sky television, led to a nine-game ban and £1,000 fine for the Cardiff player. The ban was later extended to twenty games before a legal challenge brought it back to nine and the fine down to £60.

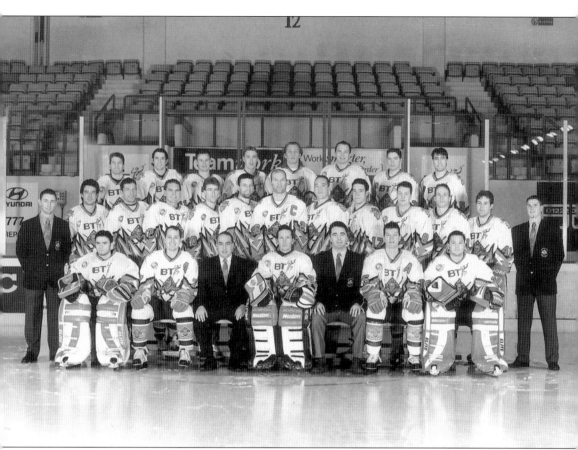

The tenth anniversary season Devils line-up. From left to right, back row: Vezio Sacratini, Neil Francis, Peter Smith, Jason Stone, Ian Cooper, Marty Yewchuk, James Manson, Doug McCarthy. Middle row: Jason Ellery (equipment), Steve Moria, Ivan Matulik, Ken Hodge, Randy Smith, Greg Ware, Mike Ware, Brent Pope, George Swan, Steffen Ziesche, Frank Evans, Kip Noble, Rob Britton (equipment). Front row: Stevie Lyle, Doug McEwen, Andy French (manager), Frank Caprice, Paul Heavey (coach), Shannon Hope, Jason Wood.

Former NHL centreman Ken Hodge Jr arrived in November, marking an upturn in Devils' fortunes. He scored two assists on his debut – a 3-2 overtime win at Nottingham. Hodge came to Britain with a fine heritage – his father, Ken, had played 978 NHL games over fourteen seasons.

Another important mid-season arrival was Canadian forward Steve Thornton, shown here (left of picture) on his debut against the touring University of Manitoba in December 1996, with David Stetch. The game ended 3-3.

Discipline in Superleague's first season was described by the much-respected *Ice Hockey Annual* as 'a disaster area'. The Yewchuk affair (see page 88) was just one example, although fewer penalties were called than in the previous season's Premier Division. Fighting remained a central part of the game, as demonstrated here when Cardiff visited Sheffield Steelers.

Ivan Matulik catches Sheffield Steelers netminder Piero Greco out of position to score one of his 32 competitive goals this season. The forward line of Matulik, Hodge and Thornton proved the decisive weapon in Cardiff's sprint to the inaugural Superleague title, which saw them finish four points clear of Sheffield.

The Thornton, Hodge, Matulik line celebrates a goal.

Thornton (right of picture) scores another past Manchester Storm goalie John Finnie at Storm's 17,000-seat arena, as ex-Cardiff defenceman Stephen Cooper looks over his shoulder. John Lawless's Manchester joined the Superleague elite after just one season in the old Division One.

High-flyer – Marty Yewchuk leaps over Manchester netminder John Finnie at Cardiff. Devils clinched the Superleague title with a 6-4 home win over Storm on 20 February 1997.

Ian Cooper, seen here in action against Sheffield Steelers, was the club's top British scorer – but down in eighth place. Sheffield avenged their league defeat by beating Cardiff in the play-off semi-final. Instead of the traditional Wembley weekend, Superleague held the semis a week before the final, all the games being played at Manchester's Nynex Arena.

Captain Mike Ware celebrates the first Superleague title, in a season which also saw Cardiff players fill four of the six All-Star team places – Lyle, Noble, Matulik and Sacratini. Jason Stone was named British defenceman of the year. Ware left the club in the summer of 1997, after his brother Greg had been released.

The close-season conveyor belt also took away a trio of Brits in Neil Francis, James Manson and Jason Wood, as well as Randy Smith and Peter Smith – who moved on to coaching Cardiff's development side the Rage, in the British National League. New names in 1997/98 included Peter Ekroth, a veteran Swedish international defenceman, whose experience and physical presence proved useful.

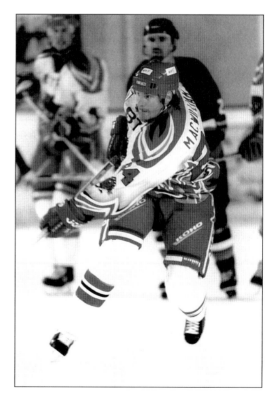

Mike MacWilliam arrived from the International Hockey League with a reputation as a short-tempered enforcer. The thirty-year-old stood 6ft 4in tall, weighed 16st 6lb, and quickly became one of the Superleague's most feared players. He missed much of his first UK season through injury, however.

Stevie Lyle was giving North America another try, this time with Plymouth Whalers, the Junior A team of the NHL's Detroit Red Wings. His absence led to the signing of American netminder Derek Herlofsky (above) from the American Hockey League (AHL). The twenty-six-year-old ended the season as Superleague's top goalie, with a goals-against average of 2.3 per game. He was desperately unlucky in the play-off final at Manchester, however, as the puck bounced off the back of his skate to give Ayr Scottish Eagles a 2-1 overtime win.

Another new name from the AHL was fast-skating winger Ian McIntyre. He had a relatively quiet debut season, with 13 goals and 18 assists in 64 league, cup and play-off games, but would become more prolific in later campaigns.

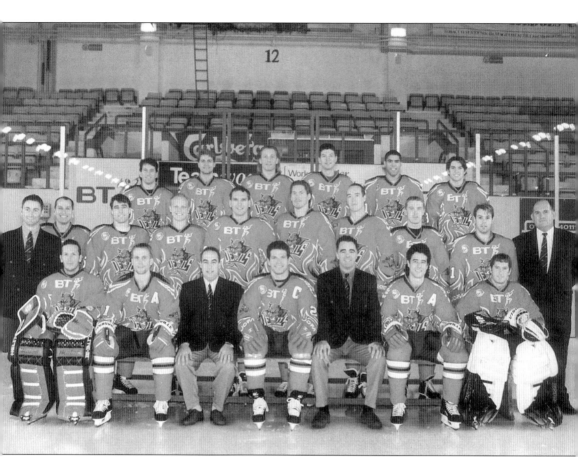

The 1997/98 squad. From left to right, back row: Vezio Sacratini, Tony Circelli, Ian Cooper, Shannon Hope, Ian McIntyre, Neil Francis. Middle row: Jason Ellery (equipment), Doug McEwen, Doug McCarthy, Steve Thornton, Ken Hodge, Mike MacWilliam, Brent Pope, Jason Stone, Kip Noble, Owen Jenkins (assistant manager). Front row: Frank Caprice, Frank Evans, Andy French (team manager), Ivan Matulik, Paul Heavey (coach), Steve Moria, Derek Herlofsky. Italian international Circelli was another new name in the squad. This was his only season in a Devils shirt.

The club was disappointed that, as defending league champions, they were not admitted to the prestigious European Hockey League – their small 2,500-seat rink was quoted as the reason for their exclusion. At the end of the season, the rink was sold to developers and leased back on a three-year contract, in the hope that a proposed new arena in Cardiff Bay would be ready by then. They rarely filled their little rink this season, however – crowds averaged just 2,146, a fall of fourteen per cent on the previous campaign.

Doug McCarthy, pictured here with his ice skates and in-line rollerblades (he was a top name in North American roller hockey during the summer), suffered a serious eye injury from an accidental high stick during a Benson & Hedges Cup match against Bracknell. It was feared the damage to his eye socket could end his career, but he returned before the end of the season. He left at the end of the campaign to join Phoenix Mustangs in the West Coast Hockey League in the USA.

There's little room for brotherly love in hockey – as Stephen Cooper found out, when his Manchester Storm side visited Cardiff. Here, Ian (right) comes off best in a clash of the Coopers. Devils' 7-1 victory over Storm in December was their biggest win of the Superleague season. Ian left Cardiff in acrimonious circumstances in the summer of 1998, claiming he had been strung along before his release. After considering offers from several clubs, including Phoenix, he joined London Knights.

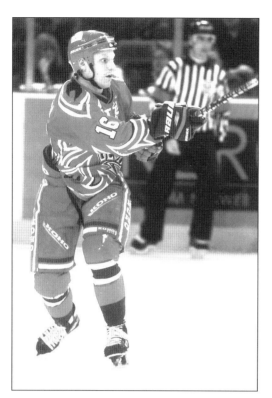

Steve Thornton was Cardiff's top scorer on their way to a third place finish in the Superleague. He scored 34 goals and 45 assists in 66 competitive matches.

Long-serving defenceman Shannon Hope received a testimonial game and announced his retirement at the end of the season, aged thirty-five. Already running a successful design and manufacturing business, Hope's Shine Dog company went on to supply playing shirts to many of the major clubs in hockey and other sports. He also took on the role of commercial manager for the Devils.

There were plenty of new arrivals for the 1998/99 campaign, some more impressive than others. Kory Mullin (right) never lived up to expectations and played only 20 games before returning to North America. Merv Priest (below left), British-born and Canadian-trained, proved a better long-term acquisition when he arrived from Basingstoke Bison, while Martin Lindmann (below right) was one of the season's stars – a dependable and steadying presence on Cardiff's blue line.

Mario Simioni proved popular with the fans. He ended the season at fourth place in the Devils' scoring charts, while top honour went to veteran Steve Moria. Simioni, however, had the distinction of scoring Cardiff's first Superleague overtime winner. His goal, assisted by Ian McIntyre, gave Devils a 2-1 win over Manchester Storm on 13 December. It was the first for the club since the new Superleague rule which required sudden death overtime at the end of a drawn league match.

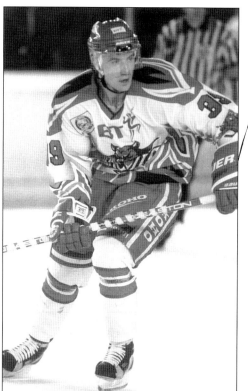

Derry Menard (left) was another newcomer who had a disappointing season in Cardiff, while young Finn Saku Eklof (right) showed much promise after joining the Devils when he came to study at a university in Wales.

Stevie Lyle returned to replace Frank Caprice, and ended the season as the league's third-best netminder, just behind team-mate Derek Herlofsky. Lyle's save percentage was 91.7, while the American bettered him with 92.3.

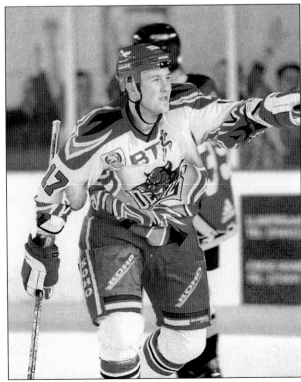

The Welshman Nicky Chinn came home from Sheffield Steelers. One of just four British-born and trained players in the twenty-one-man squad, Chinn ended the season on a high note, with a hat-trick in Cardiff's 5-0 semi-final win over Manchester in the Sekonda play-off championships. He also scored the winner for Great Britain in the crucial world championship win over Slovenia.

Another of the Welsh players, long-serving defenceman Jason Stone, scored his 100th goal – a feat which took him all of ten years. The celebrations were short-lived for the twenty-six-year-old, however – he was soon sidelined for several months after breaking his leg in a home game against Ayr.

Doug McEwen became the first man to play in 100 Superleague games, and enjoyed a fundraising testimonial game into the bargain. His own all-star team, the Running Bears, featured several ex-Devils and his own brothers.

Derek Herlofsky got his international call-up when Team USA drafted him for their world championship Pool A qualifying tournament. Pictured here in his national strip, Herlofsky played a major role in Cardiff's achieving runner-up spot in the Sekonda Superleague and going all the way in the play-offs.

Cardiff hosted a quarter-final group in the International Ice Hockey Federation's (IIHF) Continental Cup, along with top sides from Slovenia, Poland and Hungary. Devils had a miserable tournament, winning just one of their three games and having players thrown out four times – including captain Ivan Matulik twice, both for slashing. Matulik is seen here on the attack. In domestic competition, he was the club's second highest scorer, after Moria, with 23 goals and 33 assists from 62 games. Moria boasted 26 and 36.

Discipline was a problem in domestic hockey, too. Coach Paul Heavey received a written warning after a mass brawl following a home defeat by Nottingham Panthers, while the season also saw multi-game bans for Nicky Chinn and Mike MacWilliam.

MacWilliam was Sekonda Superleague's most penalised player of 1998/99, with 141 penalty minutes, an average of 4.41 per game. Pictured here in fighting form, the big defenceman was a different man off the ice – a Christian, he organised gifts for underprivileged children at Christmas, and played Santa for young fans.

After a 5-0 semi-final win over Manchester Storm, Devils faced Nottingham Panthers in the final, now at its regular home in Manchester. *Above:* Kip Noble (right of picture) takes a tumble during the final, which saw a 2-1 win for Cardiff; Ivan Matulik scored both goals. Noble had another great season, and was the only Cardiff player in the league's all-star team. *Below:* Netminder Derek Herlofsky only lost his shut-out 12 seconds from time, when he was beaten by a Mark Kolesar shot.

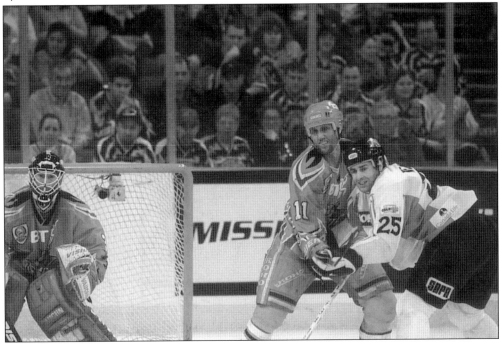

A sometimes difficult 1998/99 season could hardly have ended on a higher note for captain Ivan Matulik. After the trauma of the Continental Cup, he bounced back to score a hat-trick in a 6-3 win at Nottingham, which had briefly put Cardiff on top of the table. His two goals in the final were even more satisfying.

The management were happy too. Coach Paul Heavey (left) and manager Andy French get their hands on the play-off trophy, in front of delighted Devils fans at the Manchester Evening News arena.

Six

Hard Times
1999-2001

One of many new faces in Cardiff's ranks for the fourth Superleague season, 1999/2000, was defenceman Aaron Boh, seen here keeping Bracknell's Paxton Schulte in the dark. Boh was released early for 'disciplinary reasons' in a season which saw discipline become a major problem throughout the league, prompting the chief referee and other officials to resign.

New arrival Todd Gillingham (left) with team-mates during a period break in a pre-season challenge game against mighty CSKA Moscow. Also pictured, from left to right, are Ivan Matulik, John Brill, Derek Herlofsky and Stevie Lyle, with Steve Moria standing. Moria scored Devils' only goal in a 4-1 defeat.

Niklas Barklund was another new arrival whose stay was short. He was replaced by former Ayr defenceman Alan Schuler, who went on to have a superb season – one of the few bright spots in a largely miserable campaign.

Todd Gillingham was a hard man to pass, as shown here against Manchester Storm. His physical style came at a price, however – he topped the club's penalty table, with 264 minutes in 56 games.

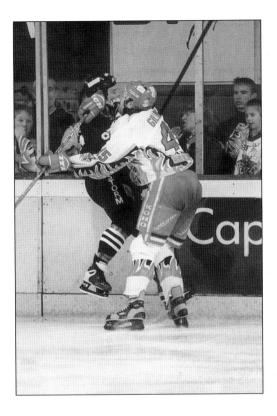

Patrick Lundback was another big signing, but he earned himself a suspension early in the season, which unfortunately coincided with Boh's dismissal and a shoulder injury to influential defenceman Darren Durdle. On top of that, assistant coach Peter Ekroth returned to Sweden – and it was still only December.

Veteran forward Steve Moria kept producing the goods. Seen here celebrating a goal against London Knights, Moria passed the 1,500 points mark for the club in a 6-2 win over Bracknell Bees in the Benson & Hedges Cup, and finished the season as Cardiff's third highest scorer.

Darren Hurley was the only additional signing before the January transfer deadline. He is seen here squaring up to London Knights hard man Barry Nieckar.

Young Jonathan Phillips became the fourth
Welshman in the team, when he was called
up from the organisation's B team, Cardiff
Rage, this season playing in the English
League. He was given little ice time, but
scored a goal in the Sekonda play-offs.

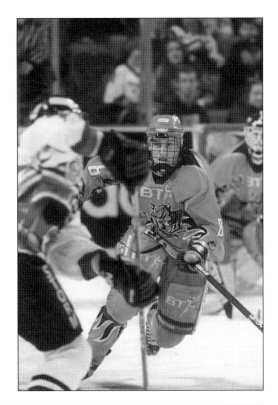

Merv Priest had a useful season, recording 10 goals and 20 assists in 58 games. He is seen here
in a post-match interview.

EUROPEAN ICE HOCKEY
1999
CONTINENTAL CUP

LADA **TOGLIATTI**   LYON **HC LIONS**

BT   CARDIFF **DEVILS**   NOTTINGHAM **PANTHERS**

22ND/23RD/24TH OCTOBER 1999 - WALES NATIONAL ICE RINK

CONTINENTAL CUP
CARDIFF ★ CAERDYDD ★ WALES ★ CYMRU

ICE HOCKEY   IIHF

22ND OCT	12.00 NOTTINGHAM v LADA 17.00 CARDIFF v LYON
23RD OCT	13.00 LADA v LYON 18.00 CARDIFF v NOTTINGHAM
24TH OCT	14.00 NOTTINGHAM v LYON 19.00 LADA v CARDIFF

OFFICIAL PROGRAMME £2.50

Cardiff again hosted a group in the Continental Cup, this time with Lada Togliatti of Russia, Lyon Lions of France and Nottingham Panthers.

Ian McIntyre in the thick of the action, with Oleg Davydov and Arthur Oktyabrev, in front of the Russians' goal during the last match of the tournament, which would decide the winners. Lada won 8-2.

Devils' Nicky Chinn causes trouble for Nottingham (and ex-Cardiff) defenceman Brent Pope. Cardiff beat Nottingham 5-3 in the Continental Cup, although Panthers had surprised everyone by defeating Lada 8-6 in the opening game. In the Benson & Hedges Cup, Cardiff beat Nottingham 6-1 away and 7-1 at home in the quarter-final, while in Superleague, honours were shared – each team winning their three home games.

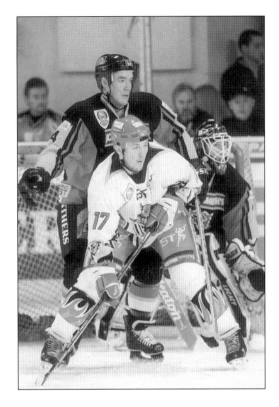

Lada Togliatti's assistant captain Oleg Davydov receives the Continental Cup trophy from John Jones, of Devils' sponsor BT. Cardiff's Stevie Lyle was voted best netminder of the tournament, thanks in part to a 100 per cent save record in the penalty shoot-out competitions held at the end of each match.

Devils' long-serving Welsh defenceman Jason Stone hinders an attack in an away match at London Knights, who went on to win the play-offs. British players were by now finding it harder to make an impression in the big league, and this would be Stone's last season with Cardiff.

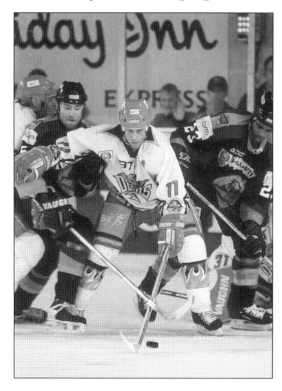

Frank Evans continued to be an influential figure in defence. He is pictured here thwarting a Sheffield Steelers attack. Sheffield won all three of their Superleague games in Cardiff this season, and two of the three against Cardiff at home – the other was tied. They also scored a 5-0 win over Devils in the play-offs.

Vezio Sacratini was one of the few Cardiff players to enjoy a good season, although he didn't see the funny side of this hooking play on a visit to Manchester. Sacratini performed well with the Italian national team in their successful Pool A play-off campaign and was Devils' equal highest scorer, along with Steve Thornton, registering 30 goals and 36 assists in 58 games. Thornton recorded 34 goals and 32 assists in 57 games.

Overall, though, it was a poor season by any standards. Here, Derek Herlofsky tries to stop a close-range shot from Bracknell's PC Drouin. A 3-1 home defeat by the Bees on 4 March 2000 condemned Cardiff to seventh place in Superleague, their lowest finish in any division.

The merry-go-round of summer comings and goings saw the return of Mike Ware for the 2000/01 season after three years away. The big man would end the season with just 3 goals and 12 assists from a total of 52 games and with 203 penalty minutes.

Among the nine new arrivals was defenceman Rick Strachan, who signed from Basingstoke Bison of the British National League. These dressing room shots were taken during the first period break of a pre-season challenge game against BNL's Peterborough Pirates.

Clayton Norris – a hard-hitting right winger in the Ware mould – was signed from Newcastle. In 60 competitive games he would score 9 goals and 17 assists, and was by far Cardiff's most penalised player of the season, with 310 minutes – an average of more than five minutes per game.

Kip Noble, widely regarded as the best offensive defenceman in the British game, returned to Wales after a year with Sheffield Steelers. He ended the season as the club's fifth highest scorer, with 11 goals and 25 assists and just 14 penalty minutes from 61 games. Noble is pictured, left, with another new signing Rick Kowalsky, one of three arrivals from Hampton Roads Admirals of the East Coast Hockey League (ECHL). Kowalsky's season was curtailed by a shoulder injury in September, which meant he played just eight games.

A new centreman was John Parco, one of Kowalsky's Hampton Roads team-mates the previous season. Parco had played in Britain before, having spent the 1997/98 season with Ayr Scottish Eagles, helping them to a grand slam of league, play-off and cup titles. For Cardiff he scored 13 goals and 15 assists in 55 games.

Another new centre, Jamie Hanlon, arrived via the German league. Hanlon showed promising form early on, but Devils management thought otherwise and he was released in October. His departure followed an unfortunate incident in a game at Nottingham on 6 October, when he was struck in the face by the puck while on the bench, breaking his nose. Cardiff lost the match 5-4.

Completing a trio of arrivals from Hampton Roads Admirals was defenceman Dwight Parrish (pictured), while off-the-ice signings included former Commonwealth light heavyweight boxing champion Nicky Piper in the role of marketing manager.

Left: The most significant off-ice appointment was the return of Doug McCarthy, as director of hockey, following Paul Heavey's departure for Ayr. *Right:* Troy Walkington (right of picture) was coach, seen here with one of the big new signings, Denis Chasse from Superleague champions Bracknell Bees. The ex-NHL forward started strongly for Devils, scoring a hat-trick in a 5-5 comeback at Bracknell in September, but his career was ended by a mid-season back injury. McCarthy did not see the end of the season either – he was axed in a cost-cutting move in December, when Devils were seventh in the nine-team league.

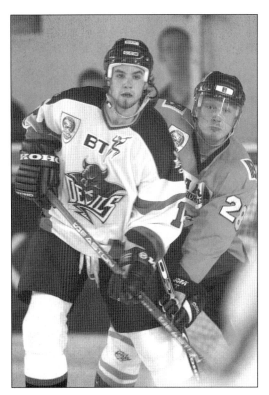

Travis Brigley, a hugely talented twenty-three-year-old forward, tipped for an NHL career, arrived from Knoxville Speed of the United Hockey League in November. His first Devils goal came in a 5-4 home defeat by Ayr on 12 November, when he also received the man of the match award. In little more than a month, he was back in North America, having scored 5 goals and 9 assists in his 12 appearances for Cardiff.

Kim Ahlroos arrived at the same time, and made his Devils debut with Brigley in a 4-3 defeat at Nottingham Panthers on 4 November. The Finn was already known to Cardiff fans, having appeared for KS Podhale in the 1998 Continental Cup, and for Newcastle Riverkings in 1999/2000. Ahlroos completed the season and made a big contribution, with 16 goals and 17 assists in his 44 competitive games.

The Devils squad early on in the 2000/01 season. From left to right, back row: Vezio Sacratini, Rick Strachan, Steve Thornton, John Parco, James Hanlon, Jonathan Phillips, Kip Noble. Middle row: Jason Ellery (equipment), Rhodri Evans, Ian McIntyre, Dwight Parrish, Clayton Norris, Mike Ware, Rick Kowalsky, Frank Evans, Steve Moria, Phillip Hill, Mark Thompson (assistant equipment manager). Front row: Stevie Lyle, Doug McCarthy (director of hockey), Mike Purcell Jones (finance director), Bob Phillips (chairman), Alan Schuler, Ivan Matulik, Denis Chasse, John Jones (sponsor), Andy French (manager), Troy Walkington (coach), Derek Herlofsky.

Steve Moria reached his fortieth birthday in February 2001, yet was still among the most feared centres in the British game. He ended the season as Cardiff's third highest scorer, with 24 goals and 27 assists in 51 games – figures eclipsed only by Steve Thornton (26 and 43) and Vezio Sacratini (27 and 31).

Moria was rewarded for his services with a testimonial game in November, when his all-star Mo-Catz took on the Devils.

The season started to pick up for Cardiff in December, when results including a 7-0 destruction of London Knights helped them up to fifth place in the league. Then January saw a double boost with two big signings. Marco Poulsen, a twenty-nine-year-old Finn, scored the equaliser on his debut at Belfast Giants on 1 February; Devils went on to win 3-2 in overtime and Poulsen was man of the match.

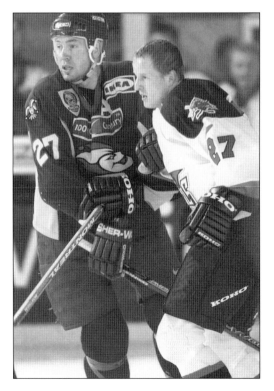

Ales Zima, a twenty-seven-year-old Czech international, was a direct replacement for the much-missed Brigley. He is seen (right of picture) on his debut against Newcastle Jesters on 10 January, when his assist on captain Ivan Matulik's opening goal helped Cardiff to a 2-1 win and a move up to fourth place.

Coach Troy Walkington guided Devils to a remarkable second place in the league. A run of 12 games without defeat, including an 8-0 hammering of Newcastle, ended with a 4-3 home defeat by Belfast Giants on 25 February.

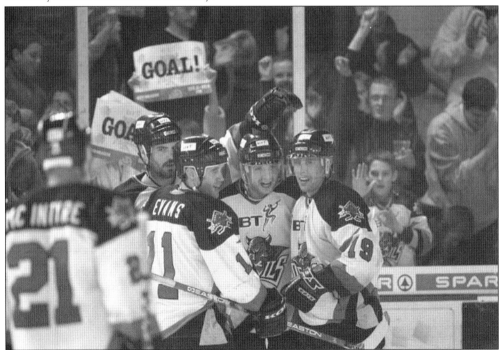

There was plenty to celebrate as Cardiff finished the Superleague season with 8 wins from 10 games, but the play-offs brought a disappointing third-place finish, meaning no semi-final berth.

As soon as the season ended, doubts were cast over the club's survival. The promised new arena in Cardiff Bay seemed no closer to reality, but with plenty of empty seats in their existing rink, there seemed little need for the bigger venue.

This report from the weekly magazine *Powerplay* on 27 April summed up the problem and highlighted indications that the whole operation could move from Cardiff.

Later, the company owning the Devils went into liquidation, with players claiming they were owed thousands of pounds. Uncertainty continued throughout the summer, and understandably almost the entire playing and backroom staff moved on. Eventually, a new company entered Cardiff Devils in the lower-level British National League, and appointed Canadian coach Ken Southwick to put together a team in less than two weeks.

The new line-up included some familiar faces from previous Devils sides, including Neil Francis, Lee Cowmeadow and Rhodri Evans, as well as some impressive imports such as Jerry Keefe, previously with Belfast Giants, and Albie O'Connell, the previous season's top scorer with Basingstoke Bison.

However, a large group of fans were angry over the actions of the previous owners, and claimed they were still involved in the new organisation. The 'Friends of Cardiff Devils' protested outside the rink and urged all supporters to boycott games.

In September 2001, ice hockey in Cardiff had become a divided sport.

Sekonda Superleague boss Ian Taylor is adamant that all nine of last season's ISL clubs will compete next season. But Cardiff's future is uncertain, Newcastle can't pay their debts and two "unfit" Sheffield directors have been banned for life. Things are not rosy.

devils' future in doubt

by Cardiff Devils correspondent Andrew Weltch

THE FUTURE OF the Cardiff Devils has been thrown into doubt, following financial losses and the continuing uncertainty over a new arena.

There are fears that the Devils could switch from the Superleague to the British National League, or move to another city altogether.

Club chairman Bob Phillips has reported losses of £250,000 for last season, with similar deficits predicted for forthcoming seasons, while Devils remain in their small 2,500 capacity rink.

Phillips wants a guarantee from Cardiff County Council that a new 8,000 seat arena will be built in Cardiff Bay, before committing himself to further losses.

The ISL has given him permission to move the franchise to another city - possibly even in mainland Europe - but the lack of any suitable venue elsewhere makes that scenario unlikely.

Another possible solution would be to build an arena of their own in South Wales - a site at Nantgarw to the north of Cardiff has been suggested.

Meanwhile, a committee has been formed to raise £250,000 to subsidise the club next season.

Cardiff Devils
Roll of Honour

1986/87
British League Division Two (Midlands)
League: winners
Play-offs: runners-up

1987/88
Heineken League Division One (South)
League: 3rd
Autumn Trophy: winners

1988/89
Heineken League Division One
League: 1st
Promotion play-off: winners
Autumn Trophy: winners

1989/90
Heineken League Premier Division
League: 1st
Heineken Championships (Wembley): winners
Norwich Union Cup: English runners-up

1990/91
Heineken League Premier Division
League: 2nd
Heineken Championships (Wembley): semi-finalists
Norwich Union Cup: semi-finalists
European Cup: quarter-finalists

1991/92
Heineken League Premier Division
League: 3rd

1992/93
Heineken League Premier Division
League: 1st
Heineken Championships (Wembley): winners
Benson & Hedges Cup: winners

1993/94
Heineken League Premier Division
League: 1st
Heineken Championships (Wembley): winners

Benson & Hedges Cup: runners-up
European Cup: quarter-finalists

1994/95
British League Premier Division
League: 2nd
British Championships (Wembley): semi-finalists
Benson & Hedges Cup: runners-up
European Cup: semi-finalists

1995/96
British League Premier Division
League: 2nd

1996/97
Superleague
League: 1st
Play-offs: semi-finalists

1997/98
Superleague
League: 3rd
Play-offs: runners-up
Benson & Hedges Cup: runners-up

1998/99
Sekonda Superleague
League: 2nd
Sekonda Championships: winners
Continental Cup: quarter-finalists

1999/00
Sekonda Superleague
League: 7th
Benson & Hedges Cup: semi-finalists
Continental Cup: quarter-finalists

2000/01
Sekonda Superleague
League: 2nd